M.E.R.R.Y.
C.H.R.I.S.T.M.A.S.

Space for Personalized Message

I0096570

Merry Christmas: A Poem of Cheer

ACRONYM POETRY GIFT SERIES

By Macarena Luz Bianchi

Designed by María Paula Gabela

To receive a free ebook, exclusive content, more wonder, wellness, and wisdom, sign up for her *Lighthearted Living* e-newsletter at MacarenaLuzB.com and check out her other poems of self-expression, books, and projects.

ISBN: Hardcover: 978-1-954489-71-4 | Paperback: 978-1-954489-72-1

Imprint

Spark Social, Inc. Miami, FL, USA, SparkSocialPress.com

Ordering Information: Licensing, custom books, and special discounts are available on quantity purchases. For details, contact the publisher at info@sparksocialpress.com.

M.E.R.R.Y. C.H.R.I.S.T.M.A.S.

A Poem of Cheer

ACRONYM POETRY GIFT SERIES

Macarena Luz Bianchi

Imprint
Spark Social Press

Dear Reader & Fellow Santa's Helpers,

Merry Christmas to you and yours! Is this your favorite time of year? May you enjoy this acrostic poem and be inspired to share your holiday cheer!

Best wishes,
Macarena Luz Bianchi

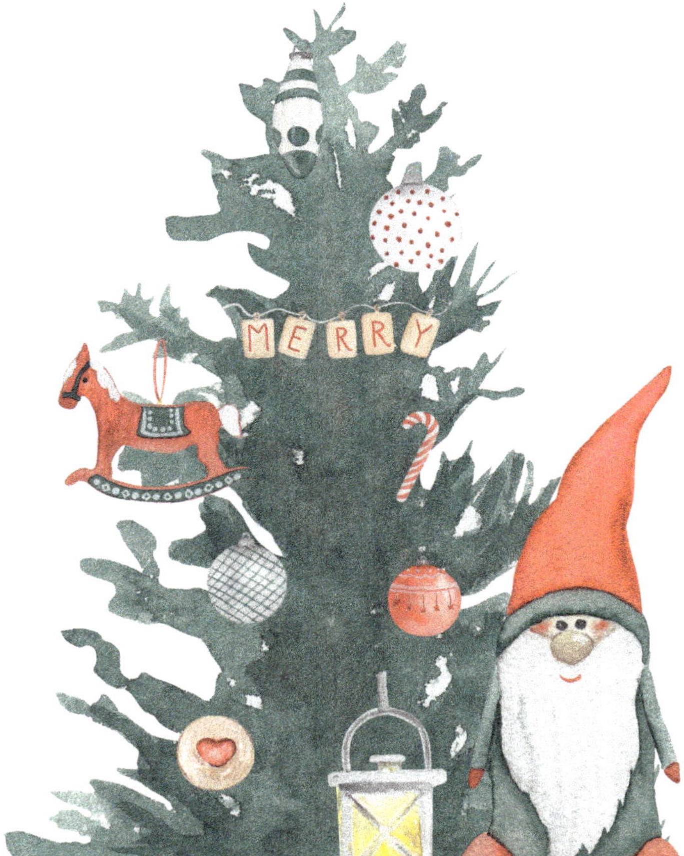
MERRY

Merry Christmas!

May all your wishes come true!

Excitement and Christmas spirit fill the air with the scent of baking, lighthearted laughter, and magic everywhere.

Reach for your holiday
decorations, gather the reindeer,
and all those you hold dear.

Ready for the nutcrackers to dance and sing while the jingle bells ring and you share your jolly good cheer?

You've waited patiently for this joyous time all year!

Celebrate cheerfully with
wonder, wellness, and wisdom!

Happy times are here again...
Enjoy gingerbread, candy canes,
and eggnog with family and friends!

Rest assured, the season is bright
with snowmen, elves, and Santa
by your side.

Inspire all to have more fun...
Even Scrooge and Grinch-like moods
will lighten up.

Sing carols around the tree
and under the mistletoe
if you're lucky.

Together, thankful and peacefully...

MERRY

Make merry memories as you laugh with ease.

Appreciate you
—and your presence—are the best
presents of all.

So, gaze up at the North Star shining as brightly as your generous heart.

May all your wishes come true,
and your Merry Christmas
be as wonderful as you!

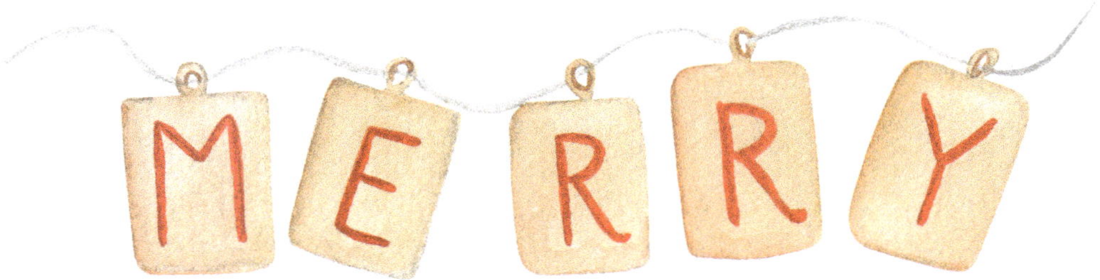
MERRY

M.E.R.R.Y. C.H.R.I.S.T.M.A.S.

A POEM OF CHEER

Merry Christmas! May all your wishes come true!

Excitement and Christmas spirit fill the air with the scent of baking, lighthearted laughter, and magic everywhere.

Reach for your holiday decorations, gather the reindeer, and all those you hold dear.

Ready for the nutcrackers to dance and sing while the jingle bells ring and you share your jolly good cheer?

You've waited patiently for this joyous time all year!

Celebrate cheerfully with wonder, wellness, and wisdom!

Happy times are here again... Enjoy gingerbread, candy canes, and eggnog with family and friends!

Rest assured, the season is bright with snowmen, elves, and Santa by your side.

Inspire all to have more fun... Even Scrooge and Grinch-like moods will lighten up.

Sing carols around the tree and under the mistletoe if you're lucky.

Together, thankful and peacefully...

Make merry memories as you laugh with ease.

Appreciate you—and your presence—are the best presents of all.

So, gaze up at the North Star shining as brightly as your generous heart. May all your wishes come true, and your Merry Christmas be as wonderful as you!

Thank you, Dear Reader!

Get Inspired & Stay Connected

To receive a free ebook, exclusive content, more wonder, wellness, and wisdom, sign up for her Lighthearted Living e-newsletter at MacarenaLuzB.com and check out her other poems of self-expression, books, and projects. ✨

Your Feedback is Appreciated

If you like this book, please review it to help others discover it. If you have any other feedback, please let us know at info@sparksocialpress.com or via the contact page at MacarenaLuzB.com. We would love to hear from you and know which topics you want in the next books. 🌻

About the Author

Macarena Luz Bianchi has a lighthearted and empowering approach and is affectionally considered a Fairy Godmother by her readers. Beyond her collection of gift books and poems, she writes screenplays, fiction, and non-fiction for adults and children.
She loves tea, flowers, and travel.

Subscribe to her Lighthearted Living newsletter for a free ebook and exclusive content at MacarenaLuzB.com and follow her on social media.💕

Macarena luz Bianchi

Gift Book Series

ACRONYM POETRY COLLECTION

- *Anniversary: A Poem of Affection*
- *Be My Valentine: A Poem of Love*
- *Congratulations: A Poem of Triumph*
- *Friendship: A Poem of Appreciation*
- *Get Well Soon: A Poem of Comfort*
- *Happy Birthday: A Poem of Celebration*
- *Intimacy: A Poem of Adoration*
- *Sympathy: A Poem of Solace*

POETRY COLLECTION

- *Dear Dad: A Poem of Appreciation*
- *Glorious Mom: A Poem of Appreciation*
- *Gratitude Is: A Poem of Empowerment*
- *Gratitude Is: Poem & Coloring Book*
- *The Grateful Giraffes: What is Gratitude?*

Also available for children and in Spanish:
Colección de Poesía I.